UNDERGROUND HOMES

UNDERGROUND HOMES
HOMES
LOUIS WAMPLER

Revised Edition

A FIREBIRD PRESS BOOK

PELICAN PUBLISHING COMPANY
Gretna 1998

First edition, April 1978
Second printing, June 1978
Third printing, November 1979
Fourth printing, March 1980
Fifth printing, May 1980
Revised edition, November 1980

Library of Congress Cataloging in Publication Data

Wampler, Louis.
    Underground homes.

    Bibliography: p.
    Includes index.
    1. Earth sheltered houses.   I. Title.
TH4819.E27W35 1980   690'.8   80-18701
ISBN 0-88289-273-8 (pbk.)

Manufactured in the United States of America
Published by Pelican Publishing Company, Inc.
1000 Burmaster Street, Gretna, Louisiana 70053

Contents

UNDERGROUND HOMES

Introduction

My interest in underground homes developed some years ago, when I started receiving high utility bills for heating and cooling my house. Each subsequent month's gas and electric bill intensified this interest. Occasionally I would notice a newspaper article describing the great energy savings to be gained by living underground; these articles whetted my appetite to learn more about subterranean building.

A search for reading material revealed that books or articles on the subject were very scarce. There were some treatises written by architects, but these were very hard to find and difficult for the average person to understand. There are now some good publications on the subject—most of which are listed under *Reference Material* at the end of this book—but while a few are easy to read and follow, most are written in technical language, often with formulas incomprehensible to nonscientists.

It occurred to me early on that there was a need for a book specifically intended for the layman. I hope that this book, the result of research I conducted while planning my own underground home, serves that purpose. I have attempted to assemble the results of my reading—and of practical advice gleaned from talks with builders and other experts—and to state them in simple language in a format that answers all the questions people most commonly ask about an underground home: Is it always dark, damp, and musty-smelling? How long will it stay waterproof? How do you repair leaks in the roof? And how do you rid the interior of excess humidity? The chapters deal systematically with each matter you need to consider when planning your home, and address the specific concerns of potential underground home owners.

The most basic piece of information to remember about underground building is that, about ten feet down, the earth is at an almost constant temperature. Taking advantage of this natural phenomenon in your construction can reduce energy consumption considerably. Surrounding a house with soil accomplishes this goal in two important ways: It moderates the extreme temperature of the outside air, and it reduces temperature loss or gain caused by strong winds.

Because underground construction is so new, most people are hesitant to undertake it. (The universal nature of these qualms may also be apparent when you ask a mortgage company about financing.) The most serious barrier preventing the popularity of underground homes seems to be psychological: A lot of people—in my experience, especially women—simply do not like the thought of living underground. There seems to be a natural tendency to think of an underground home as a place where it is always dark and damp. But it is perfectly possible to avoid these conditions. I try to emphasize building methods that will eliminate them and to suggest compromises combining features of standard homes with special features unique to underground structures.

This book is intended to satisfy the curiosity of those of you who have considered building and living underground. It should alert you to some important issues—desirable features to include and pitfalls to avoid—which you should keep in mind when you discuss construction plans with a builder. Of course nobody can talk you into living in an underground home if you are not so inclined, but the increasingly high cost of energy certainly justifies giving the matter some serious thought. I hope that this book will provide you with enough answers and insights to make your decision.

If you have no psychological barriers against subterranean living, you should begin now to think about such matters as the choice of a lot, the type of structure, strategies for dealing with moisture problems, methods of insulation, and exterior design and landscaping. You can begin your deliberation with a study of this list of advantages and disadvantages of underground homes compared to conventional houses.

Advantages

Costs significantly less to heat and cool

Quieter than surface homes

Safe from tornadoes and strong winds

Less dust in air to breathe

Fire insurance less costly

Safer from burglars, etc.

Practically no upkeep cost for exterior of building

Less risk of disturbing neighbors with such activities as piano playing, using a skill saw, parties, etc.

Disadvantages

Sometimes as much as 10 percent more expensive to build (although costs can be 25 percent *less* than for surface houses in areas where builders are already familiar with subterranean construction)

Moisture problems can plague you

Scarcity of windows for light to enter

No back yard level with the house

Figure 1
Good example of an underground house built into a low rolling hill. Drainage is away from the house and from the front and both sides. The efficient removal of water from around an underground house is extremely important. Water with the opportunity to linger or be held up around a structure may eventually find some sort of entrance. It may only be a small amount of water over a long period, but it may be just enough to cause mold and mildew. The key to preventing moisture problems is keeping the soil against the outside walls free of excess moisture.

Lot or Land

The most favorable kind of lot is one that slopes down toward the street or road. In this situation the structure can be built back into the hill with the front exposed. This gives the appearance of the front of a standard house and also provides a good place for light to enter (fig. 1).

Since there are not enough slopes or hills for everyone to use in building subterranean homes, flat lots should also be considered. Most people prefer what is called a berm type of structure when building on a flat surface. Simply stated, a berm is a structure built on the surface with soil or earth piled around and on top of it (fig. 2). When covered, a berm structure raises the earth level above the existing grade.

Figure 2

This berm structure is excellent for removing water quickly. Some builders have success with flat roofs, but in order to give the drainage a boost the roof should be slanted a little (one inch per foot or more) if it won't interfere with your design features. The slant can be from front to rear, towards both sides, or both from front to rear and to the sides.

Figure 3

Side view showing slant running from front to rear.

Front view showing drainage toward both sides.

Corner view showing drainage from front to rear and to both sides.

If the structure is built straight down in the ground, beneath the existing grade and on a flat surface—like a large basement—it is called a chamber (fig. 4).

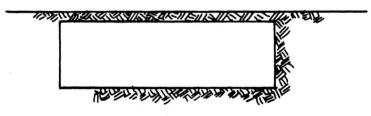

Figure 4

There are some real advantages to living in this type of structure. The main advantage is that of energy saving, which is the primary motivating force behind underground homes in the first place. This kind of house is able to take maximum advantage of the relatively constant temperature found eight to ten feet beneath the surface. If the higher portions of the structure are properly insulated, heat from the television and lights, along with body and motor heat, will probably be sufficient without any backup heating system. In the summer, when it is scorching hot on the surface, the homeowner will be relatively comfortable, enjoying the cool mass of the good earth.

All this sounds wonderful, but there are some real drawbacks. A chamber type of structure complicates your problems with both moisture and appearance. All household water and wastes will have to be pumped from the lower grade of the structure. This can be done, of course, but rest assured that the day will come when the pump (or electricity) will fail, and serious problems will develop quickly. Visualize what you would find upon returning home if a small waterline had ruptured during your absence.

Figure 5
A new neighborhood swimming pool? No, just a break—in the washing machine hose, dishwasher hose, or bathroom— while the electricity was off and the fail-safe system failed.

The next potential problem is water—either percolating rainwater or groundwater—entering from outside. Suppose you live in an area where the water table is high and you have a very rainy season. Your home might be surrounded by water, and, if there is a leak, things are going to get wet in the house immediately.

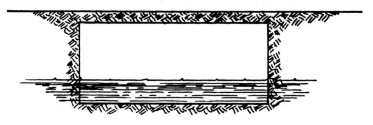

Figure 6
High water table will doom your living quarters because a leak is bound to occur somewhere.

If you live in an arid part of the country you probably will not have to worry, and if you live in a very wet area you are probably already fully aware of the hazards of a high water table. The difficulties in decision making arise in those vast areas of the country separating the two extremes. The best way to determine the water table where you live is to check first with the U.S. Geological Survey, which usually keeps records that can help you (this service is free). Check with your neighbors and see how deep their water wells are. This information is helpful, but it's not the final answer: the surest way to discover the elevation of the water table is to drill a hole about twenty or thirty feet deep and gauge it through the rainy season. This test can save a lot of heartaches. Even if your neighbor's well indicates that the water table is sixty feet deep, you might have a small water aquifer located just a few feet below the surface on your property. It may be that the aquifer fills up only during the rainy part of the year . . . just enough to flood your home. The point is, if you excavate and build during the dry part of the year you may be sadly disappointed when the first rains come. The test hole is not expensive and can be done with an auger bought at a hardware store, six-foot sections of ¾-inch water pipe, and two pipe wrenches.

Figure 7
Drilling with a hand-operated auger to test for a high water table.

If you are like many people, you are wearing the road out driving back and forth to your lot just to dream about your home. Digging your test hole will give you a further reason to go. A word of caution: don't try to dig this test hole in one day. It's worse than moving soil with a shovel, especially when you run into clay and you're ten feet deep or lower. Get ready for a big improvement in the muscle tone of your arms, shoulders, and stomach.

As a side benefit of checking the water table, digging the hole will give you an opportunity to check the depths of the different kinds of soil in which you or your builder will be digging. Soil types can vary greatly even at shallow depths. Take five small jars with you when you go to dig, place a small amount of each new type of soil in a separate jar as you encounter it, and label the jars according to the depth at which you found the soil. For example, one label might read "Red clay, three feet to six feet."

Why do all this? First, you'll learn the soil composition before the excavation starts. What if you encounter solid rock at a depth of six feet? You can move over and see if you can find a place where you don't encounter rock. This knowledge can save a lot of time and expense. Also extremely important is the information you gain about the water table. You may want to dig several test holes for a thorough test of the prospective building site. Save the jars and plot the location of the holes if you dig more than one. If you have a builder do the excavation, he will appreciate the information.

If there is a choice in the matter, build into a hill. If it is necessary to build on a flat lot, build a berm—or at least a modified berm (fig. 8), a structure built only partially below the existing surface. If you have a leaky waterline, at least you won't drown trying to save things in your home.

Figure 8

It should be clear that *gravity flow of liquids* from an underground home is a very desirable feature. In the modified berm in figure 8, gravity flow of liquids can still be attained if the sewer line or septic tank is low enough. The modified berm structure is desirable in that it is lower in the earth than a berm and has the advantage of the fairly constant temperature found in the lower levels.

The type of soil on the lot may require that you increase the size and depth of your footing. Normally, however, the soil type is not a serious problem except in one case: never attempt to build a subterranean home on land that has been used as a fill. This is because there is a tremendous amount of weight on the footing of a subterranean home, and a fill area probably won't be able to support it. Rough, washed-out land is fine, since you are going to be moving and changing a lot of the dirt anyway.

If you are building in clay, you should haul in sand and place it next to the structure, because clay will expand when wet and can exert enormous pressure on the walls, causing structural damage.

Structure

FOOTING

Whichever structure type you use for your home, it must be built on an adequate footing. To get a rough idea of the importance of the footing, think of the weight it must support. If you have a structure fifty feet by fifty feet with eight-inch concrete walls, the walls alone would weigh 160,800 pounds (note that concrete weighs 150 pounds per cubic foot). Add to the walls the weight of an eight-inch slab roof, an additional 251,250 pounds. Then add the weight of eighteen inches of soil on the top, another 375,000 pounds (soil weighs 100 pounds per cubic foot). The total weight on the footing would thus be 787,051 pounds, or 393 tons. There may be openings for doors, windows, etc., which would reduce the weight a little, but the point is that the weight on the footing of a subterranean home is far greater than that of a conventional home. So don't spare or skimp when building the footing. There are good books on the proper construction of the footings, including the correct use of reinforcing steel (see *Reference Material*).

The size of the footing required depends on the weight it will be supporting and the type of soil on which the house is being built. The purpose of the footing is to enable the soil to support great weights without giving. If there is any giving, there will be cracks in the walls, an uneven floor, and other problems. Builders rely on experience to determine the proper size of footings, but if you have no expertise in these matters you may want to use the kind of method computed in textbooks. The load-carrying capacities of different soils are shown in the following table:

Soft clay	1
Wet sand or firm clay	2
Fine dry sand	3
Hard, dry clay or coarse sand	4
Gravel	5
Hardpan or shale	6
Solid rock	10

The number to the right of the soil description indicates the number of tons per square foot such soil will support. An example will illustrate the use of the table. Take a basic structure measuring fifty feet by fifty feet. The walls are eight-inch poured concrete and there is an eight-inch slab roof. On top of the roof lie eighteen inches of soil. We need to determine the weight of one linear foot of the structure, including the weight of the wall, roof, and soil. One linear foot of a wall eight feet high would weigh 804 pounds (8 feet high x .67 feet thick x 150 pounds per cubic foot = 804 pounds). Assume that the weight of the roof is evenly distributed around the walls; this means that one wall would support one fourth of the slab roof. The total weight of the slab roof is 251,250 pounds, one fourth of which is 62,812 pounds. Since we want only the weight supported by one foot, divide this weight by 50, the number of feet in our wall. This calculation comes to 1,256 pounds.

Now add the weight of the soil (100 pounds per cubic foot). The total weight of the soil would be 375,000 pounds. Dividing this by one fourth gives us 93,750 pounds; dividing by 50 (the length of the wall) comes to 1,875 pounds. So the weight on one linear foot of the footing would be 804 pounds for the wall, 1,256 pounds for the roof, and 1,875 pounds for the soil, a total of 3,935 pounds—or 1.96 tons—for each linear foot. The footing must be able to support this weight. A footing twelve inches wide in soft clay would not be ample to support the weight; it would need to be widened to twenty-four inches. A twelve-inch footing in wet sand or firm clay would, however, be sufficient since this soil will support two tons per square foot. Note that these figures do not take into consideration any supporting beams or inner supports—they are given here only to demonstrate the use of the table.

If you use other materials (such as concrete blocks) for your walls, the calculations are essentially the same except for the weight of the blocks and the roof. The table below provides standard weights of various materials.

Weights	*Lbs./cu. ft.*
Concrete	150
Cinders (dry)	45
Charcoal	12
Soil	
Clay (dry)	63
Clay (damp)	110
Silt (moist and packed)	96
Sand and gravel (wet)	120
Gravel (dry)	104
Sand (dry)	90
Water	62.4

You may wonder whether or not the footing should be reinforced with steel. I would say a very definite yes. As you know, concrete has very high compressive strength but relatively low tensile strength (compressive strength is the ability to support heavy weights without breaking or crushing). The concrete normally delivered by ready-mix companies is called a 2,000 mix. This means that the concrete can support 2,000 pounds over every square inch of its surface without breaking or crushing. Most of the underground homes in my area use a 3,500 mixture of concrete, which would support 3,500 pounds per square inch before breaking or crushing.

Remember that the concrete itself must be supported by the soil under it. Driveways provide a good illustration of

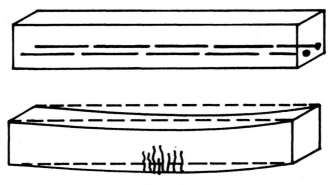

Figure 9

Pressure on the top of a beam exerts compression on the top of the beam and tension (stretching) on the bottom. Concrete has high compressive strength but low tensile strength. As pressure is applied at the top of the beam, there is a strong tendency for it to crack or break at the bottom because of its low tensile strength. Placement of reinforcing steel near the bottom of the beam (usually within two or three inches of the bottom) greatly increases its tensile strength.

this principle; the soil under a driveway supports the concrete. When a heavy truck drives over a sidewalk, chances are that the sidewalk will crack. If the same sidewalk were reinforced with steel bars, the chances of a crack would be lessened considerably. If your footing had the same amount of weight on each foot, there would probably be no need for reinforcing steel. But because of windows, doors, etc., some parts of the footing will necessarily be carrying more weight, and when extra weight is placed on a particular part of the footing you run a risk that the footing will crack. Because of the low tensile strength of concrete, reinforcement steel in the footings is therefore recommended.

When you're ready to begin building, start by determining the boundaries and setback lines. Usually boundary stakes have been driven in the corners of platted or recently conveyed land; these corner stakes can be used for boundary determinations. If there are no stakes, hire a surveyor to determine the boundaries of the property.

If you are building on a hill or slope, do some rough excavating in order to level the building site somewhat before you start construction (fig. 10).

After the rough excavation is completed, locate the proposed front corner of the structure and drive a two-by-four stake at that point (point A). Now drive another stake at a point that will be the depth of the structure (point B). A line from point A to point B should be parallel to the outside boundary line. Place nails in the centers of these stakes so the measurements will be from the nail in point A to the nail in point B (fig. 11).

Now drive a two-by-four stake six feet from point A on a line toward point B. Another stake should be driven eight feet from point A and ten feet from point B. Call this point C. The triangle BAC is a right triangle. The other corners of the structure can now be located easily.

Figure 10

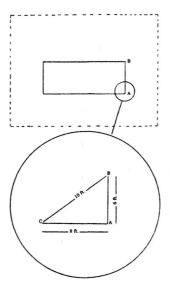

Figure 11

After the corner stakes have been located, set up batter boards (fig. 12). These batter boards are usually set about four feet back from the corner stakes in order to provide room for final excavation. The batter boards must be level. Now stretch strings over the batter boards so that the strings cross exactly over the boundary stakes. A plumb should be used to ensure an accurate point of crossing. Cut notches in the batter boards so that proper location of the strings on the batter board will be recorded in case they are moved or broken during excavation.

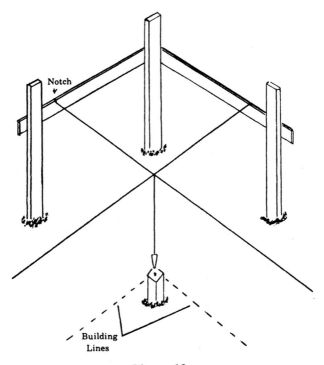

Figure 12

The corner stakes can now be removed for final excavation of the footing since accurate location can be judged from the batter boards.

The footing should always be below the frost level. When water and soil freeze there is considerable expansion and when thawing follows contraction occurs. This phenomenon is known as heaving. If the footing is not below the frost line, the structure will likely suffer damage from the heaving process. Use weather bureau information to determine the maximum depth of the frost line and be sure that the exposed area of your structure has a footing below the frost line.

Figure 13 gives a cross-sectional view of the typical composition of a well-constructed footing. Builders in your area may not use as much reinforcement steel as shown since the footing in this example would withstand a lot of pressure in unstable soil. Always follow the advice of a reputable local builder.

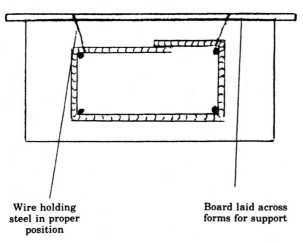

Wire holding   Board laid across
steel in proper   forms for support
position

Figure 13

The horizontal reinforcement steel bars should be as large as your budget will allow but under no circumstances smaller than five-eighths of an inch in diameter. The collars holding the bars can be bought preshaped, or you can shape your own. The collars should be spaced closely enough to keep the horizontal bars level—about every three to five feet.

The steel in the footing should be positioned so that the bottom part is about three inches off the excavated area. The steel should be supported by wires attached to a board placed across the forms. Never attempt to support the steel with stakes. Stakes will rot or rust out and eventually the steel in the footing will rust because of moisture and weaken to such a degree as to be of no practical support for the structure.

The vertical rods (fig. 14) should not be positioned until the concrete stiffens a little, usually after about thirty minutes. Note the shape of the key joint. Such joints are very important in ensuring a tight seal between the footing and the base of the wall; they are formed by beveling two-by-fours and positioning them when the concrete is wet. Sometimes these two-by-fours are difficult and time-consuming to remove. As a result, the building industry has come up with a new type of key joint (fig. 15). This new method utilizes a rubber-like material about half an inch thick and four inches in depth. It comes rolled up like a large leather strap, and is unrolled and placed about two inches down in the footing when the concrete is wet, with the other two inches sticking out to form the water seal in the wall when it is poured. This method is fast, effective, and easy.

When you build your house, don't forget to consider ingress and egress locations for the various utilities. Probably the first time you need to consider this is when you

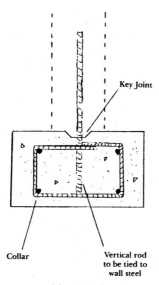

Key Joint

Collar

Vertical rod
to be tied to
wall steel

Figure 14

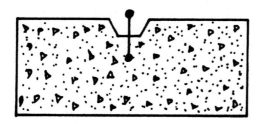

Figure 15

pour your footing. Your sewer drain will probably need to go through the footing. The other utility items such as electricity, water and phone can enter almost anywhere (the garage entrance is one good location). When making your plans, be sure to provide footing in the areas where you will have pilasters and fireplaces as well as at utility exits.

Figure 16

Underground home with a large part of the house exposed to the elements. Note too that there are a large number of windows, which let in a lot of cheery sunlight but thereby tend to defeat somewhat the purpose of saving energy by going underground. Fifteen times more heat is lost through windows than through walls in surface homes. This loss can be offset, however, by using double pane (insulating) glass and properly placing it on the south side of the house. People considering living underground must reach a compromise on the matter of fuel conservation vs. appearance vs. natural light. Each family differs, but it is important to decide in advance on your style of underground home and not to change your mind after the building starts.

WALLS

The walls of an underground home are similar to the basement walls of a large house. They are generally of two types: poured concrete walls, and walls of concrete blocks. Poured concrete walls use reinforcing steel both vertically and horizontally. Concrete block walls also use reinforcing steel for added strength and stability. There is no doubt that concrete block walls are easier to build because you can put the wall up one block at a time, but there is something about poured concrete that symbolizes strength, and strength is of the essence in underground houses. Which to use is of course up to you.

Concrete cures best when the temperature is between 70 and 80 degrees fahrenheit. It should be kept moist for seven days if possible. Concrete will harden to about 90 percent of its eventual hardness during the first seven days. Proper curing will increase the compressive strength to three or four times that of improperly cured concrete.

Whichever wall you choose, don't forget to use the correct size and number of pilasters. It is a good idea to place pilasters on the inside of the structure where the walls will stand so that they can be covered as part of the internal walls. Pilasters should be placed inside in this way because it is easier to waterproof a flat wall on the outside than to contend with a series of pilasters sticking out of a wall. Another idea is to make closets, bookshelves or storage space where the pilasters are located in order to camouflage them somewhat (fig. 17).

Concrete experts advise you to place pilasters at intervals anywhere from twelve feet to twenty-five feet to ensure wall stability. If, when you decide on your floor plan, you place the pilasters at points where there will be internal walls as suggested above, you will simultaneously gain stability and camouflage the pilasters.

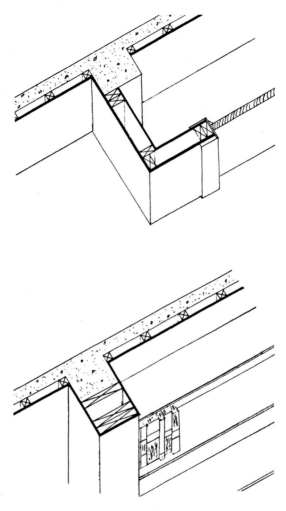

Figure 17
Top drawing shows how a pilaster can be cam-
ouflaged somewhat by being made part of the
internal wall. Bottom drawing illustrates use
of a pilaster as one end of a bookcase.

If you are building a berm on a flat surface, the lateral pressure on your walls is not nearly as great as it is on walls built into a hill (a structure built into a hill can and usually does have considerable lateral thrust against its walls). Most of us have seen retaining walls built to keep soil from washing down on the sidewalk. Unless these retaining walls are built properly, they will yield to the force of the earth and water and commence to lean.

Figure 18

Cross section shows results of lateral force against an improperly constructed retaining wall. Gravel and drain (or weep holes) relieve much of the pressure exerted by water.

The same thing can happen to the walls of an underground home unless they have proper support.

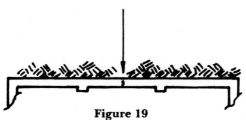

Figure 19

Inadequately braced wall will crack and probably leak.

The purpose of pilasters is to resist the powerful forces exerted on the walls. Because of the strong force exerted by the earth and water on the walls of a downhill underground home, many people have started building curved walls.

Circular walls support themselves without pilasters and provide excellent water drainage on their outside surfaces. Instead of the water running head on into a straight wall, it circles around the gentle curve of the structure and drains off at a distance.

If you have serious doubts about the holding force of the wall of your home being built into a hill, change the plans so that the house will face uphill. If done properly, the walls of the house will now have little lateral force on them compared to those of a house facing downhill.

If you are pouring your roof, the top of the wall should have a key joint similar to that in the footing. Poured walls usually have reinforcement steel bars placed vertically and horizontally on twelve-inch centers. The reinforcement steel bars should extend at least two feet out of the top of the wall so that they may be bent and tied to the steel in the roof. The reinforcement steel at the corners and where the bars meet should overlap at least two feet for good bonding.

It should be noted that there are more economical ways to build walls than with poured concrete or concrete blocks. The walls of some underground homes are being built using methods learned from the builders of swimming pools. After the excavation is done, the footing is poured. After that, a network of steel is set up (just as in the construction of a swimming pool) and then a mixture of concrete (or dry material and water sprayed separately) is blown against the earthen walls. Although this gunnite method of wall construction is convenient, it presents

Figure 20
Circular or round wall can withstand great lateral thrust of earth without cracking. Percolating water is easily drained around the outside of a structure by following the contour of the wall.

Figure 21
Cutaway view of an underground home facing either uphill or to the side with a yard area cut out of the uphill side. There is little lateral pressure on any wall of the house. The drainage will be good if there is adequate sloping from the front area. The disadvantage of this type of structure is that soil will cover only two sides—the lateral thrust problem has been solved at the expense of exposing more of the house to the elements.

some serious problems. There is no drainage at the bottom of the structure, and no waterproofing or insulation on the outside. If you live in a part of the country with a rather dry and mild climate, this type of construction might nevertheless be satisfactory, but I would think about it for a long time before I set the building in motion.

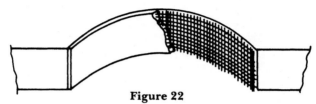

Figure 22
Walls of an underground home being built using the gunnite method.

There are other materials currently being used for the walls of underground homes, including timber. If you are considering using something other than concrete you should try to visit some underground houses in your area built of the materials you're considering to evaluate them. Decide if you like what you see and inquire about the energy savings.

SLAB FLOOR

Before the slab floor is poured, several things ought to have been accomplished. First, the under-floor plumbing should be completed. Gravel or coarse sand should then be placed over the various plumbing pipes and tubes. In many surface homes, heating ducts are placed under the slab floor. Although you may like heat coming from such floor ducts, it is recommended that ducts be placed above the slab floor of an underground home because, if moisture should enter the ducts, serious moisture problems would arise inside the structure. The top of the gravel or sand would be nearly level with the bottom of the slab. If you are going to insulate your slab, the vapor barrier should be positioned over the sand or gravel; the insulation should then be laid, then the steel wire; finally, the concrete should be poured. The concrete should have a compressive strength of 3,000 psi with a minimum thickness of four inches, and the slab should be reinforced with welded wire.

Figure 23
Cutaway shows makeup of a typical slab floor. Note insulation on the front edge of the house.

ROOFS

The roofs of subterranean homes are generally of three types: slab roofs, prestressed concrete roofs, and conventional roofs. The slab roof is made of solid concrete which has been poured in place around reinforcing steel after forms have been positioned. It is extremely heavy and must be supported by concrete or steel beams, usually poured simultaneously with the roof. A slab roof is an excellent idea, but the forms and bracing required to pour the concrete are costly.

How much and what size steel to use in the slab roof is an extremely technical question and one on which expert advice should be sought. The stress caused by the weight of the concrete—and eventually the soil—is tremendous. The distance of the roof span between support points is critical; the greater the span, the greater the strength needed. The span can be reduced by proper planning of load-bearing partition walls. Such walls must be strong (much like the outside walls), and they must be built on footings adequate to carry the roof weight.

If you use precast forms for the roof, there will be a space of between eighteen and thirty-two inches from the top of the wall to the top of the form. This space must be filled so that soil can be placed against the structure. Concrete blocks are usually used to fill it even if you have poured concrete walls eight feet thick. The blocks permit easy exit of vents, etc.

Roofs made from prestressed concrete forms have a lot of strength and don't have the great weight of slab roofs. However, precast forms present other problems. They usually have to be placed in position by use of a crane and there are cracks between the sections after they are in position. These cracks must be sealed so that no moisture can enter from the top. One method of handling this problem is discussed in the chapter on waterproofing. As mentioned above, a good feature of prestressed forms is that they are set on a couple of legs which provide a good place for chimneys, pipes, etc., to exit. This is better than going through the top of the roof (fig. 24).

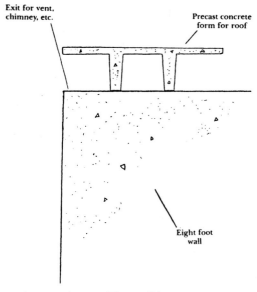

Exit for vent, chimney, etc.

Precast concrete form for roof

Eight foot wall

Figure 24

The other type of roof observed on bermed homes is the same as that found on conventional homes. If you choose a conventional roof, use ample insulation above the ceiling just as you would in any ordinary house. A house with this roof is not a true underground home—it might be called an earthen-jacketed house. It has several important advantages, discussed in the chapter on standard roofs.

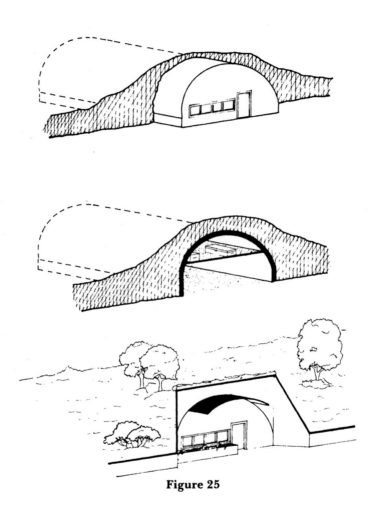

Figure 25

A most intriguing new idea is a structure shaped like a shell, half barrel, or quonset hut (fig. 25). After the footing is in place, dirt could be piled and shaped so that it becomes the form over which concrete is poured. Reinforcing steel should be placed before the concrete. One or both ends would need to be left open so that a front-end loader could enter to remove the dirt. Two major problems would arise with this method: a great volume of dirt would have to be moved, and the concrete would have to be pumped or lifted with a crane and bucket to reach the height of the shell. A structure in this shape should be extremely stable and very easy to waterproof. I don't know anyone who has tried this technique, and without such a pioneer people seem to be afraid to attempt it. Think about it—you may be the pioneer.

Suppliers do manufacture large corrugated steel arched structures which might serve your purpose very well. They also have information on sizes, strengths, and other concerns. For confidence in the strength of your structure, it is hard to beat the oval or round shape—for both the walls and the roof.

Waterproofing

If subterranean homes are to be acceptable, they must be free of excessive moisture. The first kind of moisture to be eliminated is extrinsic moisture—moisture or water coming from the outside in the form of percolating rain and groundwater.

Let's start at the bottom of the structure. A drain needs to be placed around the outside of the footing. This is usually done with perforated plastic pipe and about six inches of pebbles or chat above and beside the pipe. The pipe should slope about two inches every twelve feet for proper runoff, although some builders say sloping one inch every twenty feet is sufficient. This drainpipe will prevent a large buildup of water against the walls which would surely cause leaks and which would exert a tremendous pressure on the walls, possibly leading to cracking. If the water table is high, the drain would help water run off before it could enter the house (figs. 26 and 27).

A likely place for a water leak is at the juncture of the wall and the footing. Because the footing is wider than the wall, that little ledge is a good place for water to collect and eventually leak through to the interior. To avoid this, place

Figure 26
Proper drain around structure.

Figure 27
If water is a serious threat, place sand or rocks nearly up to the surface and back from the wall twelve inches.

a little concrete along this troublesome juncture. This will prevent the flexible waterproofing material from bending sharply and becoming leak-prone.

Concrete, whether in the form of a poured concrete wall or a concrete block wall, will not be waterproof. Waterproofing material of some kind needs to be placed on the outside of the wall. Hot tar and saturated felt seem to be favorite impervious materials for waterproofing outside walls; most people use hot tar over and under saturated felt paper. The outside walls are not difficult to waterproof since the water will percolate downward, enter the drainpipe, and be carried away from the structure.

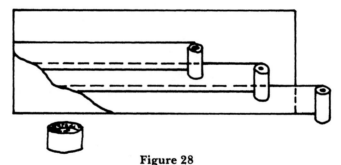

Figure 28

Hot tar and felt paper are used to waterproof outside walls.

Some people persist in thinking that concrete is waterproof, but you should remember that it is not an impervious material. Although water moves through concrete at a very slow pace, it will eventually penetrate. If this moisture moves through the concrete walls of an underground home and stays trapped there, mold, mildew, and bad odors will surely follow. This is exactly what you want to prevent. Concrete companies do have a waterproofing chemical which can be added to concrete when it is mixed at a cost of about one dollar per cubic yard. (Probably by the time you read this, the price will have doubled!) It's well worth the price, but there will still be some moisture penetrating the concrete.

The most challenging waterproofing job will be the roof, which needs to be constructed so that it will be waterproof not only now but twenty years from now. A leak in the roof of an underground home can be extremely hard to repair. In the first place, there may be trouble even locating the source of the leak. You may know the place where the water is dripping through the ceiling, but the actual spot where the water is leaking through the roof may be ten feet away. When the exact location is known, a considerable amount of dirt must be removed before the repair work can commence. Because of the problems involved in repairing a leaky roof, it is highly advisable to make every effort while building to assure a roof that will be leakproof now and for years to come.

If you have a concrete slab roof, serious leaking problems are usually not too great. Most of the people in this area use hot tar and saturated felt on the roof. How many layers you use depends, to a degree, on what your budget will stand. But if there is any part of the house on which you ought to go all-out, it would be the roof. Since most builders put three to four layers on ordinary flat surface roofs, this should be a minimum guide for roofs of underground homes. Other materials used for waterproofing the roof are large sheets of plastic and sheets of butyl rubber.

A more difficult waterproofing problem is presented when the precast forms are used for roofing. The problem is greater because, when the forms are laid in place, there is a crack where the sections join. In this situation most people simply put the tar and felt paper over the structure as if the cracks were not there. This may not cause a problem if the precast forms are placed close together, but if they are not pushed together and there is a crack of any size between them, trouble will be forthcoming. It seems that a good way to handle this is to place some sort of bridge over the crack, regardless of the size of the crack. This will support the impervious material when it is positioned and the area over the crack will be elevated a little, allowing water to drain away from the crack. You may have your own ideas about what material to use for the bridges; a mixture of cement, sand, and small round rocks might be a good one to try. It might also be wise to use wire reinforcement in this strip of concrete, following the crack from one end of the structure to the other. After the crack is bridged, continue with the waterproofing just as you would with a slab roof.

Another idea is to lay down a bead of a good sealant on both sides of the crack, then place a metal band over the crack for a bridge. The metal band will act as the bridge and the sealant under the band will prevent the intrusion of water if there is a leak through the waterproofing material (fig. 29).

Some good underground home builders recommend a layer of concrete on top of the precast forms. The economics of building the house have a definite impact on

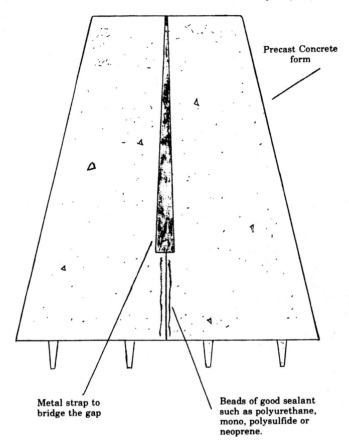

Precast Concrete
form

Metal strap to
bridge the gap

Beads of good sealant
such as polyurethane,
mono, polysulfide or
neoprene.

Figure 29
Cover cracks where double tees are joined.

how far you can go in waterproofing your roof. If your budget will stand a layer of cement, by all means put one on.

Assuming the exterior walls and roof have been adequately waterproofed, you can now concentrate on moisture problems in the interior of the structure. First, before the slab floor is laid, make sure that vapor barrier material is positioned so that the concrete slab floor will not be a source of excessive moisture.

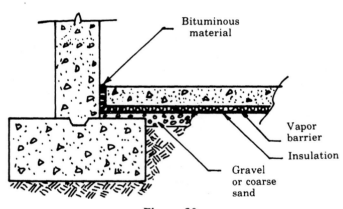

Figure 30
Properly constructed slab floor.

Even if the structure is waterproofed on the outside and bottom, there may still be excessive moisture problems. Inside a house, large amounts of moisture are created by cooking, washing and drying clothes, and showering. The areas where these activities take place need exhaust fans to remove the moisture.

Even with the precautions you have now taken, you may still have moisture from hot air hitting cold walls. As you probably know, warm air will hold considerably more moisture than cold air. When hot air comes into contact with a cold concrete wall, it is cooled. Since the cold air will not hold as much moisture, droplets of water are formed on the walls. The temperature at which the vapor turns to liquid is called the dew point.

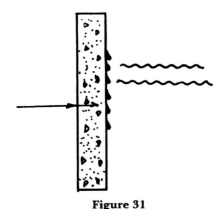

Figure 31
When warm moist air hits a cold wall, moisture forms.

Wet walls are pretty common in unvented basements and cellars. If the structure is vented, the excess moisture is usually carried off. However, underground dwellings can't be vented like concrete cellars because with vents you would lose a lot of the benefit of being underground. If you have insulated your structure, you probably won't have much of a dew point problem. During the summer months the drying process of an air conditioner probably will be sufficient to take care of the excess moisture—and circulation of outside air will also carry off moisture. In the winter, the problem is not as acute since the cold air being heated to warm the structure is quite dry anyway. If you are seriously plagued with dew point moisture, you may need to install a dehumidifier.

Insulation

Insulation will generally pay for itself in a few years by saving fuel costs and by eliminating the need for large and expensive heating and cooling equipment. Your primary concern when considering insulation is: how effective are the various materials available, and which kind should be used on underground homes.

Most manufacturers now use the R-value rating on their insulation products (the "R" stands for resistance to heat transfer). This rating makes it easy to compare insulation. If the product you are looking at gives only the "C" or "U" rating, you need to convert this to the R-value in order to make comparisons. The letters "C" and "U" are interchangeable. To convert them to the R-value, divide the number given into one. For example, if the "U" value is stated as .5, the R-value is 2 (1 ÷ .5 = 2).

Most insulation manufacturers now use the NAHB label. This means that the insulation has been tested by an independent laboratory and that the product meets the thermal performance specification stated on the package—that is, the R-value is what the label claims it is. If a product has no NAHB label, you must accept the manufacturer's label or shop for a different manufacturer.

The following chart gives some idea of the R-value of the materials shown:

Material	R-value	
Batt		
Cellulose fiber	4	per inch of thickness
Mineral wool	3.8	per inch of thickness
Loose fill		
Mineral wool	3.3	per inch of thickness
Vermiculite	2.0	per inch of thickness
Board or rigid		
Urethane (foamed in place or preformed)	5.8	per inch of thickness
Polystyrene	4.5	per inch of thickness
Glass fiberboard	4.3	per inch of thickness
Wood fiberboard	2.90	per inch of thickness
Plywoods and softwoods	1.25	per inch of thickness
Plaster, stucco, brick	.20	per inch of thickness
Solid wooden doors (one inch thick)	1.56	per inch of thickness
Sand-and-gravel concrete	.08	per inch of thickness
Single glass	.88	
Double glass with ¼-in. space	1.64	
Eight-inch concrete block	1.89	

Note: It would take a concrete wall twenty feet and eight inches thick to give you an R-value of 20. It would take less than four inches of urethane. To put it another way, it would take a concrete wall 6½ feet thick to give you the same R-value as one inch of urethane.

Most of the time you will have the option of using several kinds of insulation. If you do, make a comparison using the cost per unit of resistance. Do this by dividing the cost per square foot by the R-value. For example, if you can buy rigid insulation either in two-by-eight sheets one inch thick for three dollars or in four-by-ten sheets two inches thick for nine dollars, which is the better buy? The smaller sheet has sixteen square feet. Dividing this into the cost of three dollars, the cost per square foot would be eighteen cents. Dividing this figure by its hypo-thetical R-value of three, the cost per unit of resistance would be about six cents.

Compare that to the cost of the larger sheets, the square footage of which would be forty. Dividing this into the cost of nine dollars, the cost per square foot would be twenty-two cents. Now divide this by the R-value of six (since it is two inches thick), and the cost per unit of resistance would be about 3½ cents. So the larger sheets would be the better buy by far.

These computations can be made for all types of insulation if you know the R-value, square footage, and cost per square foot.

The R-value for soil varies from .5 per foot to as much as 5 per foot. Light, dry soil has the highest insulative value; wet, heavy soil is the least effective insulation.

Many of the underground homes existing today have no insulation other than the soil surrounding the shell. From a temperature standpoint, the walls of an uninsulated underground shell ten feet below the surface will vary from about 45 degrees to 69 degrees fahrenheit, depending on what part of the country it is located in and what time of year it is. In Fort Worth, Texas, for example, the wall temperature would vary from 63 degrees to 69 degrees fahrenheit. The variance is brought about by the influence of the surface temperature. Remember, however, that there is about a three-month lag in the temperature at a ten-foot soil depth. In other words, the wall of an underground structure about nine or ten feet deep will be coldest about three months after the coldest period on the surface.

This three-month lag gives the underground dweller a significant advantage over the surface dweller. For example, the heat from the August sun will not be felt ten feet down in the earth until about November—exactly when the surface temperature is getting cold. When surface homes require the most heating, you will be getting the maximum heat from Mother Earth. Likewise, when it begins to get hot on the surface you will be receiving maximum cooling from the earth. This phenomenon is one of the most exciting features of underground homes. Just think: when it is 15 degrees outside, a home on the surface must use enough energy to raise the temperature 50 degrees to achieve a temperature of 65. By contrast, an underground home may not need to raise its temperature at all if the walls are 65 degrees at the time. Such calculations make you want to grab a shovel and start digging (fig. 32).

In St. Paul, Minnesota, the temperature variance of the same structure would be from 45 degrees to 50 degrees fahrenheit. So whether or not you insulate your structure may well depend on what part of the country you live in. It is pretty safe to say that an uninsulated underground structure is less costly to heat and cool than a well-insulated home on the surface.

A pretty good guide to the temperature of the soil about ten feet deep in the area where you live is the water temperature map published by the U.S. Geological Survey (fig. 33).

The recommended minimum R-values for ceilings and walls for surface homes are probably published regularly in your area. These values can be used as guidelines for the amount of insulation you need for your underground home. Let's say, for example, that you live in the middle part of the United States and that the recommended R-value for the ceiling is 30 and the recommended R-value for the walls is 19. This then is the guide you should follow. The R-value of the ceiling should certainly be followed—or even exceeded—because the recommended R-value is the recommended *minimum*. The soil on top of your home will not provide you with enough insulation, so

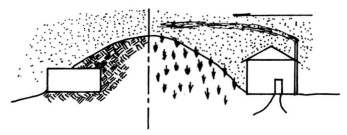

Figure 32

Comparison of heating requirements of a conventional home with those of an underground home. The surface home (right) loses substantial heat because of infiltration and energy required to keep the inside temperature at a comfortable level. The underground home (left) loses very little heat through infiltration and requires very little energy to keep the temperature comfortable inside. Since space heating constitutes about 65 percent of your energy requirements, these differences are very important.

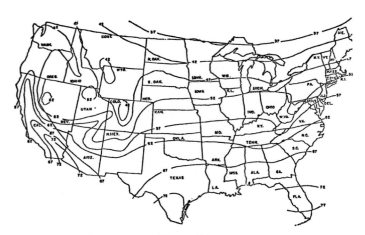

Figure 33

U.S. Geological map showing temperature of water from depths of thirty to sixty feet.

you should add more while you are in the process of building. Remember, an underground home is not like a surface home where you can go up into the attic and put down six more inches of loose fill insulation. I am assuming, of course, that you are placing the insulation on the outside of the structure.

When considering insulation for walls, note that there is a difference between underground and surface homes which should be recognized. Assuming the recommended minimum R-value for a wall is 19, the whole wall of a surface home needs the same amount of insulation since it is about as cold at the bottom of the wall as it is at the top. This is not true of the wall of an underground home. The soil near the top portion of an underground wall may be near the freezing point, but as you go down the wall toward the bottom, the temperature rises—maybe to 60 degrees. It makes good sense to use more insulation on the top portion of the wall, where it is cold. It may be that the differential would justify using two or three times as much insulation near the top of the wall.

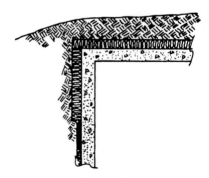

Figure 34
This cross section shows the top half of the wall with three times as much insulation as the lower half.

Another way of insulating would be to use standard insulation batts if the shell has framework inside. The insulation batts can be placed between the two-by-four studs.

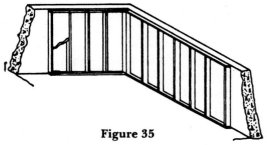

Figure 35

Cutaway showing an underground structure or shell with framework inside. Insulation batts are placed between the studs as in surface homes.

The floor may be insulated—if you so desire—like any slab floor. In the warmer parts of the country where you are not going to insulate the entire slab, you should insulate for at least two feet from the wall that is exposed to the outside elements.

Figure 36

Insulating the two feet of the slab floor which are exposed to the outside elements is very important. Otherwise, that portion of the floor will become very cold in the winter and will chill the floor throughout the room. In colder climates, you may want to insulate the whole slab; in any case, the outside perimeter should have the most insulation.

If you are building framework inside a concrete shell, you could insulate the ceiling with the standard pour-in or batt type insulation as you would in a standard home (figs. 37 and 38).

It seems difficult for some people to get used to the idea of insulating on the outside and gaining the value of the storage capacity of the massive concrete structure, yet the same people would be quick to recognize that an empty food freezer requires more energy to keep at a constant temperature than a full one. Note too, in figure 35, when insulation is placed inside, between the studs, that the entire wall will have the same amount of insulation even though the top part is much colder than the bottom. By insulating on the outside you can place more of the insulation where it is needed—near the top of the wall.

If you insulate your structure on the outside, you will probably need to use a rigid type of insulation. The insulation can be placed against the outside of the building, with soil holding it firmly in place. Be sure that the rigid insulation to be used will not deteriorate when it comes in contact with water. Check the manufacturer's specifications.

If you insulate on the inside of your structure, you can use almost any of the standard insulation materials. Remember, however, that polystyrene is flammable and that its use should probably be limited to the outside. If you are insulating inside, remember that the vapor barrier on insulation goes toward the *inside* of your house.

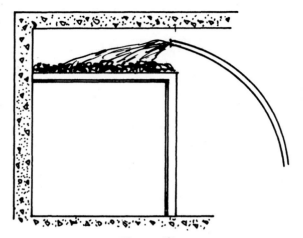

Figure 37
Insulation can be applied in the ceiling as it is
in the standard home.

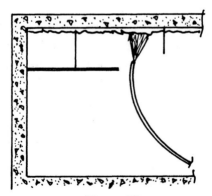

Figure 38
Spray-on insulation may be applied where the
ceiling consists of suspended panels.

Interior

How you decorate the walls of an underground home is a matter of personal preference. Some people like to leave certain parts of the house rough—with the concrete or concrete blocks showing as the surface of the interior wall. If they use poured concrete walls, some people put on a light coat of plaster and paint after the plaster dries.

Builders now have textured concrete forms that can be used on the inside walls. These forms can assume the appearance of brick or other designs. Some people frame the inside of their homes as any conventional house would be framed; finish the rooms with sheetrock, plasterboard, or gypsumboard in four-by-eight sheets; and then paint and paper as desired. What you do inside is up to you, but of course the more you do, the more it costs.

If the inside is framed and plasterboard is used, there may be a problem with the ceilings if there are some large rooms. If you have been to the lumberyard recently you know that lumber in general is costly and that long two-by-twelves for ceiling joists are extremely expensive. One way to avoid such expense is to use the hanging type of ceiling with drop-in sections. These now come in panels that are compatible with homes and not just commercial buildings. Shorter pieces of lumber could be used for ceiling joists if they can be supported from the top. Ceiling support is not much of a problem if the roof is a slab. Just place the necessary hardware in the forms before the roof is poured. When the forms are removed, there will be something to which material can be attached for your ceiling support.

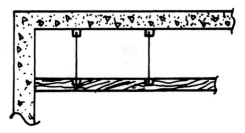

Figure 39
Cutaway showing short joists being hung from hardware sticking out from a poured roof.

Ceiling support is more difficult when precast sections are used for the roof. These forms are sometimes called "double Ts" (or double tees) because if you view a section from the end it looks like two Ts (fig. 40).

Figure 40

Some builders drill holes in the base of the stem of the T, insert lead or plastic in the holes, and then put a lag screw through the lumber into the lead or plastic to hold the joist. There seem to be serious flaws in this method of attaching the joists. I think that when the weight of the sheetrock is pulling down there will be considerable trouble with the holding strength of the lead or plastic in the holes. Also, those precast forms are engineered quite precisely, and I would be very hesitant about boring any holes in them for fear of diminishing their strength.

Perhaps a more satisfactory way of supporting the joists might be to use metal straps which could be inserted between the precast forms before the waterproofing is done on top. The metal straps would give you something to which the ceiling joists could be attached for support (fig. 41).

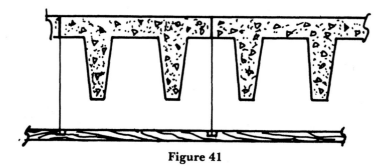

Figure 41

There are some excellent glues on the market that will hold great weights. Wood and metal can be glued to concrete. This might be an excellent method of attaching weights from the ceiling where there are long spans.

Internal noise can be bothersome in underground homes. Noise originating from the outside is not a problem—when you are surrounded by soil you may not even know that it's raining. Since you are also surrounded by concrete, however, it may sound as if you are in a gym when you talk or produce other noises. There are good sound deadening boards available, but probably the most economical way to restrict the transmission of noise is with the use of thermal insulation in conjunction with slit-stud or staggered-stud walls (figs. 42 and 43).

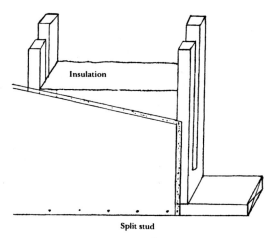

Split stud

Figure 42

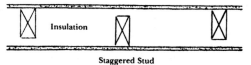

Staggered Stud

Figure 43

For the slit-stud wall, saw about one half inch in the two-by-fours before erecting. The slit should be sawed to within three inches of each end of the stud. The idea is to create an air space in the studs so that the vibration in the walls will be substantially reduced. Regular thermal insulation is installed between the slit or staggered studs if you are using this method.

Of course, all internal walls will not need to be designed for such drastic sound reduction. I'd recommend that the walls of all bathrooms and of those rooms in which loud noises are generated should be designed this way. Any areas in which peace and quiet are important to you should have this wall construction.

Carpeting is also excellent sound absorption material. Compare the noise in an old office building with tile floor to that in a more modern, carpeted building. In the old office building it seems as if the slightest noise is audible at the end of a block-long hallway.

If you are using a suspended ceiling the final sound absorber might be acoustical panels.

When finishing walls and ceilings, remember that lack of light can be a real problem and that light-colored paint and paper should be used. Fluorescent lights should also be considered since they use less electricity and provide excellent illumination.

Mirrors should be used to the extent that they fit into your decorating scheme. They give the impression that rooms are much larger than they really are. Even more important, strategically placed mirrors can reflect sunlight almost anywhere you need light. The combination of light-colored paints and paper, mirrors, and fluorescent lighting should give you plenty of light.

There are several things you can do from an interior decorating standpoint which will help relieve any negative psychological feelings about living underground. One idea is to have murals of scenes you like. Some people even place a window frame with lighted murals of outside scenes; the scenes can be changed by rolling the paper in the window frame. Another idea is to drape a complete wall to give the impression that, if you opened the drapes, you could walk out on a patio. If your budget won't permit draping of an entire wall, place drapes over what might appear to be a window. What you are trying to do here is create an illusion of being in a conventional home if that is important to you.

If you are going to paper some of the walls, use both light-colored paper and outdoor designs—birds, flowers, streams, etc. Let your own taste be your guide. The most important thing in decorating is to pick the design yourself and not to let anyone force some idea on you that you know you don't like.

Natural Light

Lack of natural light in an underground home can be a real problem because of the reduced area available for windows. In conventional houses we get our natural light from windows and skylights. These are also the sources of natural light for underground homes, but it is obviously more difficult to channel as much light underground.

SKYLIGHTS

The good features of skylights are known to all. First, they provide sunlight, which will otherwise be significantly reduced in underground homes. Skylights that open also provide good air circulation when needed and can act as escape hatches in the event of fire or some other emergency when the usual exits are blocked.

But there can be some real problems with skylights. They are the source of considerable heat loss in the winter and they radiate a lot of heat in the summer. They are noisy as the dickens when it rains or hails, and you lose a lot of privacy because of them unless you use translucent glass. They are also good places for intruders to enter and they can be prime spots for water leaks.

Most of these problems can be offset to a large degree. There are some excellent skylights on the market today with double-pane construction to minimize heat loss and gain. There are also some skylights with venetian-blind construction under the glass or plexiglass.

Figure 44
Typical skylight with the addition of venetian blind apparatus near the bottom. This creates dead air space which reduces heat loss and gain and noise and makes it possible to adjust the intensity of entering light.

This venetian-blind construction is beneficial because it significantly reduces heat loss or gain as well as noise from storms, etc. You should make every effort to install skylights that can be raised for ventilation. All skylights should be secured from the inside for security purposes.

Many people decide that, if they are going to bother to install skylights, they might as well install large ones. This can be a mistake, since small skylights can provide large amounts of light. If you are receiving too much light through a skylight, adjust the venetian-blind handle.

If you use precast forms for your roof, skylights are probably much more difficult to construct. You could cut into the precast form, but this would probably seriously weaken its strength. You might place two of the forms apart with sufficient space between them for placement of skylights. In either case, you would have to pour a concrete curbing for the skylight to sit on. This certainly can be done, but you would have to use care to properly waterproof the area where the curbing attaches to the precast form. The best way to install skylights in precast forms is to have the forms made in advance with a place left for the skylight.

The slab roof and the skylight curbing should be poured at the same time to reduce the chances of a water leak.

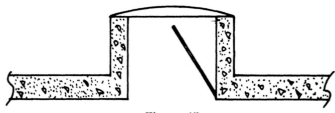

Figure 45
Skylight with trapdoor construction. These are available on the market, or you can make your own. If you do, you can build the hinged door of a light board frame with a center of plexiglass, or use a polystyrene center covered with quarter-inch plywood for a good insulation cover at night. The door could be held open with a small magnetic strip of metal.

WINDOWS

If you decide on windows in the front of the structure, face the structure in a southerly direction if possible. This will permit you to have a passive solar system by letting the sun's rays enter the windows in daytime, thereby heating the house to some degree. The amount of heat will be much greater if the sun can hit dark-colored masonry. This is easy to say but hard to do—it is difficult to find something that is made of brick or concrete and painted a dark color to put in front of a window. Dark floors or perhaps a planter box might be suitable for this purpose (fig. 46).

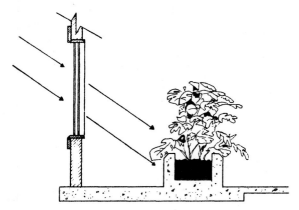

Figure 46

One caution, however: you need to be able to insulate the windows at night. A good way to insulate windows is to use insulated curtains or panels which will either slide or fold out of the way. These will not detract much from the aesthetic effect since there will probably be drapes over the windows in the usual fashion.

Windows in underground homes are placed on the front or exposed portion of the structure and ordinary construction methods can be used for their installation.

Even if the windows do nothing more than let in some light, they are worth the time and trouble. In other words, if the windows are used just for light and a view outside, with no heat gain from the sunlight, put them in anyway. After all, this is not a dungeon we are going to live in.

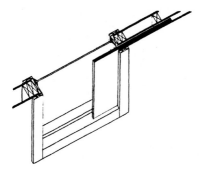

Figure 47
Insulated window panels.

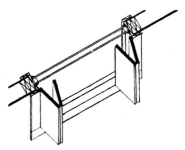

Figure 48
Another type of window panel.

Some building codes require that at least 10 percent of the floor space of a room be in window space. Sometimes this is difficult to accomplish in underground homes. If the code has such a provision in your area, see if a variance of some sort can be obtained because of the nature of your building.

As a general principle, windows should be as high in the wall as possible to lengthen the depth of light penetration. At the same time, the window should be low enough so that maximum use can be made of the sun's rays for solar heating purposes.

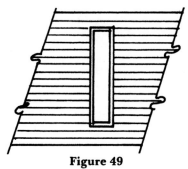

Figure 49
This window is too narrow.

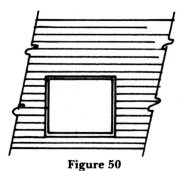

Figure 50
This one is too low.

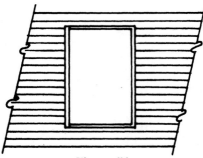

Figure 51
This window is high enough for deep penetration of light, and wide and low enough for solar heating purposes.

Heating and Cooling Systems

Standard systems of heating and cooling would certainly be suitable for underground homes. If you could move your present home underground and retain your heating and cooling system, your utility bills would immediately be substantially reduced. How much your bills would be cut is hard to tell—you hear the wildest stories about how little it takes to heat or cool an underground structure, and even by consulting the most scientific studies you won't be able to determine with much accuracy how much energy money you will save because there are so many variables. These variables include the way the structure is built and especially how much of it is exposed to the surface temperatures. Other variables are the same as apply to surface-built homes—the life-style of the occupants, etc. One family might reap tremendous energy savings living in an underground structure while a neighbor's savings could be minimal.

Homes have certain sources of heat seldom thought of as such. Some of these sources are refrigerators, lamps, televisions, and human bodies. In surface homes, there is usually so much infiltration that these heat sources don't mean much in the winter months. In an underground home, however, there is very little infiltration and such sources of heat will go a long way in helping to keep the home warm.

Even though underground homes don't need as much heat as surface homes, the heat sources just discussed are still going to have to be supplemented to get the temperature to the desired level in your home and to keep it there. You have several alternative sources from which to choose.

SOLAR

Solar energy designed to heat and cool homes is one of the most exciting topics being discussed in relation to today's energy crisis. It's exciting because it is clean, free, and exists in unlimited quantity. Harnessing the sun has generally seemed unrealistic for most people; solar heating systems for water are in clear reach of everyone, but the big obstacle seems to be capturing and storing enough of the sun's energy to heat (and cool) our homes. Underground homes make the use of solar energy for heating more feasible because such homes require less heat than conventional structures. In fact, an underground home might be heated exclusively by the solar method because of its reduced need for heat.

(a) Passive

As you are probably aware, solar heating systems are divided into two broad categories: passive and active. Passive systems are those in which the sun shines through windows, heating masonry. The masonry acts as the storage medium and releases the heat as the interior of the structure cools down. Active solar systems operate with the use of fans, pumps, switches, etc.

For a trouble-free system, passive heating is preferable—and there are no operating costs. But from a practical standpoint, passive heating is hard to accomplish. Glass windows can be built to face the sun, and they can be covered with insulated curtains at night, but the difficulty is finding the storage medium. If you can design your house so that the sun strikes a dark masonry floor, wall, or something of the kind, you have it made.

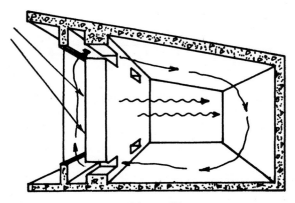

Figure 52
Thick concrete wall stores heat from the sun all day and keeps the house warm at night. However, a large chunk of concrete also blocks out light, and lack of light may already be a problem.

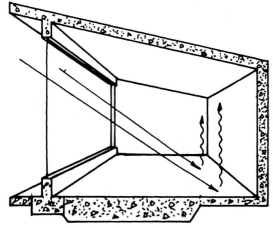

Figure 53

Lay that large chunk of concrete down and use it as a floor. Make the floor thick where the sun hits it with good insulation underneath. That, most people can live with.

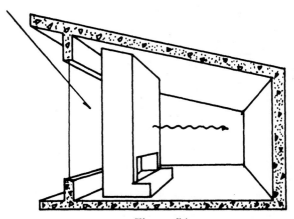

Figure 54

A massive fireplace would store a lot of the sun's heat.

It is most critical in establishing a passive solar system that your house orientation be correct. This simply requires that you face your windows in the direction that will give them the greatest exposure to the sun's rays—south. You not only need to place the windows facing in the proper direction, you must also have the proper overhang on the windows so that you don't get the full effect of the sun through them in the summer. It would take a tremendous amount of air conditioning to cool down a house in the summer when the hot sun is shining down on dark masonry inside the house; so, if you plan a passive solar system, the overhang on your roof should extend over the windows so that the winter sun will enter the windows but the summer sun will not. You need to determine the winter and summer angles of the sun where you live.

Figure 55
Sun in winter comes in at a much lower angle than in summer. Overhang of a house or window can give natural protection from hot summer sun. Books about solar energy will provide tables of maximum/minimum sun angles, or you can call your local weather office for information.

Almost without exception, you will need a booster type of heating along with the passive system. There will be days when the sun will not shine and you will need some other source of heat on those days—and on cold nights. But no matter what other heating system you install, take advantage of the free heat from Mother Nature.

One problem with the passive system is that it provides very little air movement. Because of potential moisture problems, it is desirable to have the capability of moving air in and out of each room. This concern might move you in the direction of considering an active solar heating system, which will aid in moisture removal by circulating air.

(b) Active

With an active solar system, you will need collector panels, motors, fans, and switches. One of the big problems of this system is finding a storage medium for all the heat collected by the panels. Some people use water, others use rocks, and still others seem to be working frantically to come up with a medium that will store a great deal of heat in a reasonable space. No doubt somebody will eventually come up with an idea and many of those working on the problem will wonder why they didn't think of it first.

The federal government has been awarding grants for experiments in the energy field; one experiment which is going to get a lot of attention is being conducted in Alaska, where a gentleman has a large underground storage tank for water. Solar panels will collect the heat from the sun, and electric fans will blow the hot air through the storage tank via ductwork to heat the water and be recirculated through the solar panels for reheating. The tank of water will be heated in this way all summer, and the idea is to store enough heat to last all winter—with a little help from the fireplace. Wouldn't it be something if you could store up enough heat for winter from a source that is absolutely free except for the electricity needed to run the fans?

Living underground should not necessarily be the determining factor in deciding whether or not to use solar energy. Use the same criteria you would if you were making the same decision in a surface home.

NATURAL GAS OR LIQUID GAS (PROPANE)

Natural gas and liquid gas are good clean-burning fuels with a fairly high burning efficiency. But most important of all, they are relatively inexpensive. If you contemplate using a gas system of some sort, try to put the furnace in an area—such as the garage—where the oxygen for the burner will come from outside the structure.

WOOD

People from coast to coast are talking about using wood for heating. It is a renewable resource and it has "soul." There is something about burning wood that seems to affect people—I don't know exactly why, but the feeling is good. There is a strong sentiment in favor of returning to wood as a source of heat, but I expect that its impact on our energy problem would be very small. Still, if you live in timber country and the wood is free for the cutting, why not use it as much as possible?

(a) Stoves

There is currently a strong demand for wood-burning stoves, especially some of the very efficient European brands and some good American ones. At any rate, wood-burning stoves would be excellent for underground homes, except that lack of oxygen can be a problem. Solutions might include cracking a window just a little, or—better yet—feeding the fire with outside air via ductwork.

(b) Fireplaces

Fireplaces certainly are compatible with underground homes. Historically, the fireplace has been one of the most inefficient heating systems around. The efficiency ratings vary from a minus figure to as high as 17 percent. The main problem has been that so much of the heat goes up the flue instead of entering the house. In addition, after the fire has died down late at night the warm air from the house continues to go up the flue, forcing the regular heating system to work much more than it should. In times past, little thought was given to the escaping warm house air because heating bills had not reached a shocking level.

Things are changing, however, and new solutions are being found. First, tight-fitting glass doors are now being placed on the front of the fireplaces. These can be opened or shut when the fireplace is in use. Just below the doors are small louvered panels that regulate the amount of air coming in to feed the fire. When you retire at night, the glass doors can be shut and the louvered panels closed. If the front fits tightly, the fire will die out and warm house air will not go out the flue. This is an excellent heat saver.

Another improvement in fireplaces is a design that allows the oxygen needed to fuel the fire to come from the exterior of the house and not from the warm air inside, which now stays inside. To control the fire, use the regular damper on the fireplace and another damper on the outside air source. With this system efficiency is substantially increased (figs. 56 and 57). Place the fireplace inside the house and not on the outside wall so that the mass of the fireplace can be used to store heat from fires and from sun streaming in through the windows. If the fireplace is located on an outside wall, cold will move through it to the interior.

Fireplaces are now constructed so that much of the heat which heretofore went up the flue can be extracted and saved. All sorts of heat exchangers are sold for this purpose. Some use thermostatically controlled fans to force

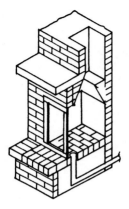

Figure 56
Example of a fireplace with air coming from outside the house. This system does not use oxygen or warm air from the interior.

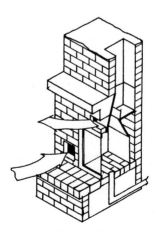

Figure 57
Another example of using the outside air. Glass doors should be used on all fireplaces.

warm air through ducts to all parts of the house. When the fireplace is not in use, the regular heating system takes over.

As a general rule, a chimney should be at least two feet taller than any part of the structure within ten feet of it. On flat roofs, the chimney should be three feet taller than the roof. This will keep you from having downdraft problems and smoke inside your home.

Fireplaces can be an excellent means of ventilating the home in the summer months when moisture buildup can become a problem. Simply open the damper and let the warmer air escape out the flue. The outgoing air will carry excessive moisture out with it.

ELECTRICITY

For years builders advertised proudly that their houses were all-electric. Such advertising has quietened substantially since utility companies have been forced to stop granting all-electric home users such favorable rates. When all-electric home owners pay for their electric usage at the same rate as other residential customers, their heating bills in winter are very high. Electric heat is very clean, and, if your heating elements are of the baseboard type, electric heat is among the quietest forms available. From a comfort standpoint, it is an extremely desirable heating source but, again, it is very expensive. If you are using wood stoves along with some passive solar system and need an occasional heat supplement, electric baseboards would be ideal. They would be relatively inexpensive to install and would be used only as necessary, so that the expense would be reasonably low.

1965   1975   1985

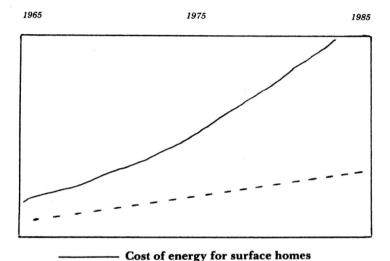

———————— Cost of energy for surface homes

— — — — — Cost of energy for subsurface homes

Figure 58

This graph compares energy costs for surface and subsurface homes. Prior to the 1970s, utility companies charged less per unit of energy as the volume increased; this method of pricing promoted the use of more energy. As the energy crunch continues, the trend is just the opposite; the more energy you use, the more it costs per unit, the theory being that this rate structure will promote conservation. As a result, surface home dwellers not only use more energy to heat and cool their homes, but the energy is more expensive per unit than that used by subsurface dwellers.

HEAT PUMP

Heat pumps have come into their own during the last few years. These units act as heaters and coolers. They have no burners; instead, they move heat (either in or out of the house) by use of a compressor and fans. A heat pump operates much like an air conditioner, except in the winter, when the process is reversed and heat is actually extracted from the outside and transferred into the house. This is the air-to-air heat pump. There is also the water-to-air system, which extracts heat from water and transfers it to the space in question, or, when cooling is desired, extracts heat from the space and transfers it to the water.

COOLING SYSTEMS

From an energy standpoint, no cooling system beats an open window with fresh air coming in at the proper temperature. Of course, this principle is recognized by everyone. Proper overhangs and shade trees can help lower energy requirements for cooling during the hot summer months. Both are discussed under other headings.

In addition to window and attic fans, the standard central air-conditioning system is excellent for underground homes. If you have ductwork for a central system, none of the ducts should be below the slab floor because of the potential moisture problem.

Standard window units would be an excellent cooling system even though they don't particularly enhance the appearance of a house. Several small units would be better than one large one so that an area of the house which need not be cooled could be closed off and its unit kept turned off.

There is a lot of talk about the use of earth pipes as an inexpensive cooling system. One recent newspaper article told of a gentleman in Texas who was building his own underground home. While drilling for water, he hit an underground cavern which blows air at a constant 68-degree temperature year round. The air was tested and found to be good fresh air. Can you imagine? That could only happen in Texas.

The idea behind earth pipes is that air from a hot house could be circulated through a pipe buried ten feet or deeper. The air would be cooled as it traversed the length of the pipe and then recycled through the house. The whole system could be operated with a small fan. It's an excellent idea, especially now that the recommended temperature for our homes is no lower than 78 degrees in the summer. The gentleman from Texas has an earth pipe supplied by Mother Nature.

It has long been felt by some that if you had a shallow water zone you could pump water up through a heat exchanger and let the water flow back into the same water formation for recycling. Fans would pull air through the heat exchanger and into the house.

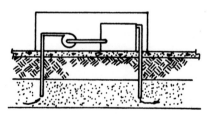

Figure 59
Air-conditioning system making use of ground water, and recycling water back into the same formation, where it will be cooled to a constant temperature.

Comparative costs of the various methods might be of some value in your selection of the backup system. Nobody questions the wisdom of utilizing a passive solar system because it is so inexpensive and trouble-free. But what is the most inexpensive backup system insofar as operating costs are concerned? It takes a little calculating to come up with the answer. The following information was provided by the Oklahoma Department of Energy:

—As we have already seen, the cost of home heating depends greatly on the type of heating fuel used. But, the cost also depends on the thermal efficiency of the home. The thermal, or energy, efficiency of a home is influenced by such items as *insulation, storm windows,* and *weatherstripping.* Adding energy saving items to a home increases its thermal efficiency.

—For example, let's analyze the heating cost of two homes in central Oklahoma. Both homes are identical in floor plan and design. Both have 1400 square feet of living area, 196 square feet of exterior glass area, and are constructed on concrete slab floors. The only difference in these two homes is the thermal efficiency.

—Home #1 has 3½ inch batt-type insulation in the exterior walls and ceiling area. The windows are single-glazed. The concrete slab is uninsulated, and the home is only partially weatherized with caulking and weatherstripping. The thermal efficiency of this home is typical of many in Oklahoma.

—Home #2 has a fairly high thermal efficiency. The walls have 3½ inch batt-type insulation plus one inch of polystyrene. The ceiling area is covered with 10 inches of blown insulation and the concrete slab is insulated with 2 inches of polystyrene. Storm windows are in place, and all windows and doors are caulked and weatherstripped.

—The seasonal heating requirement for each of these homes has been calculated using standard procedures. Home #1 was found to require 790.4 therms of heat during an average heating season, while Home #2 required just 413.9 therms because of its higher thermal efficiency.

—The seasonal heating cost for the two homes has also been calculated using each of the three heating fuels and the heat pump. Table 1 shows the actual costs of heating.

Table 1. HEATING COSTS PER THERM

Heating Fuel	Example Fuel Price	Actual Cost of Heating
Natural Gas	$2.25/1000 cu. ft.	$0.34/therm
LP Gas	$0.33/gal.	$0.62/therm
Electricity	$0.04/kw-hr	$1.23/therm
Heat Pump	$0.04/kw-hr	$0.49/therm

Based on the current prices of fuel and the cost of heat as shown in this table, the *annual* heating costs of the two homes were calculated. The annual heating costs can be calculated by multiplying the cost of heat in dollars per therm by the seasonal heating requirement of the homes in therms. The results are shown in Table 2.

Table 2. ANNUAL HEATING COSTS

Heating Fuel	Annual Heating Cost	
	Home #1	Home #2
Natural Gas	$268.74	$140.73
LP Gas	$490.05	$256.62
Electricity	$972.19	$509.10
Heat Pump	$387.30	$202.81

—Table 2 is very interesting! It very clearly shows the effect that the type of heating fuel can have on the annual heating cost. However, the heat pump is fairly competitive to natural gas heating. In areas where natural gas is unavailable, the heat pump can be a good alternative.

—Table 2 also reveals a great difference between the heating cost of the two homes. The annual heating cost of Home #1 is almost twice as much as the cost of heating Home #2. Again, this is because Home #2 has a higher thermal efficiency. From this example, we can see the value of insulation, storm windows and weatherstripping. The application of these items to a home can reduce the heating cost as much as 50%.

Before changing your heating system, check with your local utility or regulatory body to see what the price is for the particular fuel you've chosen in your locale.

If your computations show that the heat pump is very competitive, as it is in the example above, why not save money and install heat pump window units in your underground home? The only requirement would be to plug them into the wall sockets (which may need 230 volts). These should not block out the sun because special openings can be built below the windows, or can be placed on the roof or any wall except the south wall. They might not be quite as attractive as a central system and the noise might be louder inside your home. Still, this is an idea that will let you get into an underground home with little expenditure on heating and cooling systems.

Ventilation is a subject which should not be overlooked. Proper ventilation in a home assures you of sufficient fresh air for breathing, and removes vapors, moisture, odors, and gases. Unless you are building an underground home completely covered with soil except for one door, there probably will not be an oxygen problem anyway, but a forced-air heating and cooling system is highly desirable in order to be able to circulate fresh air in and out of the rooms for ventilation purposes. If you have a fireplace and gas furnace, remember to feed the flames with outside air. In the warm months, open the fireplace damper and windows. If it is too warm for this, use the central cooling unit. Charcoal filters can be used to help remove any odors.

Exterior

A man once tried to occupy an underground home without any soil or other material on top. He thought the bare concrete would make a nice place to sit, have picnics, play basketball, and enjoy other activities. I should hasten to tell you that this simply will not work. Concrete holds an enormous amount of heat or cold. In the summertime, the sun heats the concrete and it is almost impossible to cool the interior, while the reverse is true in the winter.

The more soil you can pile on top, the better off you are from a heating and cooling standpoint. But you should be aware of the tremendous amount of work involved in transferring eighteen inches of soil to the top of a building measuring fifty feet deep and fifty feet long. This would be 3,750 cubic feet or 139 cubic yards of soil. If you have ever moved soil with a shovel and wheelbarrow, you know that it's a tremendous job to move even a ten-yard dump-truck load of soil. The idea of moving fourteen such truckloads with a wheelbarrow is pretty shocking to most of us. Moving the soil with a front-end loader would be an easy job, but the roof won't support this kind of concentrated weight unless you use a front-end loader on one of those very small garden tractors. Even then be sure about the weight stress before using it. A back hoe could be used to move the soil much of the way onto the roof. Or a long but light-weight conveyor belt might be rigged to transfer the soil to the desired location; a back hoe or front-end loader could then be used to place the dirt on the belt, which could be moved as needed.

When planning your soil cover, always keep in mind that the weight of soil puts a great strain on the structure. Most people put from one to three feet of soil on top. Vermiculite or perlite mixed with soil may be used for this purpose; this mixture gives both bulk and insulation and substantially reduces the weight. However, these two products hold moisture and deteriorate; nurserymen mix them with soil and other materials for use as a potting mixture. If you live in a dry climate, you may want something that would hold moisture, but otherwise you might want to consider light material that will not. Such material might be polystyrene pellets or volcanic rock (pumice), or you might find other mixtures that would work equally well or even better.

In addition to the soil or soil mixture, you need some kind of vegetation growing on top. The roots will help hold the soil in position and the leaves will reduce the heat in the summer. What vegetation you put on top is of course a matter of preference, but the least expensive choice is probably native grass or ivy. Ivy is an evergreen vine which spreads rapidly after the first year and is an excellent ground cover. It will grow in the open sun or in shade. Honeysuckle and ajuga might also be considered. You should consult your local county agent or nurseryman on this matter.

Some underground dwellers want to use the top of their home as a lawn and plant native grass suitable to the area.

It is preferable, however, to keep all activity off the top of the structure because of potential problems with water leaks. Children, for example might dig through the soil while playing and create conditions that might ultimately cause leaks.

Other people prefer small trees or shrubs of some sort. This certainly can be done, but bear in mind that cumulatively shrubbery and small trees simply add more weight to the already heavy structure. However, a few could certainly be used to camouflage pipes and vents.

I personally favor a low ground cover practically undisturbed by man and beast. Whatever you decide on, be sure it is a plant that will grow in your area. No matter what you decide to use, remember that vegetation of some sort is very necessary to reduce the effects of the hot summer sun on the bare soil which will, in turn, heat your structure.

Without vegetation, not only will the summer sun overheat the soil, but torrential downpours will also cause soil erosion. After placing soil on top of the structure, add a lot of mulching material on top. If you are a gardener, you already know the value of mulch. It serves the same general purpose on top of underground homes. First, the mulching material breaks up the hard impact of rain and lets the water enter the soil at a slower speed than it would otherwise. This helps reduce the washing away of the soil. Secondly, a good mulch helps retain moisture already in the soil. The third benefit from mulch is that the hot summer sun will not hit the soil directly and thus will help keep the structure cool.

Expensive mulch is not necessary to do a good job. Oat straw (or other cereal straw) is probably as economical as any mulching material if you live in an area where farmers raise oats. Other good mulching materials include cottonseed hulls, peanut hulls, peat moss, leaf mold, sawdust, hops, and shredded bark. To save money, find mulching material that is made or grown in your area.

Here are some cautions to observe: Don't use mulching material that will be washed off with the first heavy rain. Don't use fresh-cut green stuff like grass clippings because a chemical reaction sets up in green grass clippings and creates considerable heat. If grass clippings are used, be sure they have been dried first. If you use fresh sawdust or bark, add nitrogen to the soil because, as these materials break down, they draw nitrogen from the soil and the newly planted ground cover will suffer. Add two to three pounds of nitrogen fertilizer to each one-inch layer of sawdust spread over one hundred square feet of the surface.

If you have a chamber type of home built back into a hill, the appearance of its front is most important because that is the only part that will be visible. Most of the underground homes in this area seem to have simply designed brick or rock fronts, usually extending from one to three feet above the top of the structure. The purpose of extending the front wall (or parapet) above the top of the structure is to keep the soil on top from washing away and to prevent water from draining into the entry area (fig. 60).

One significant problem exists with this type of construction. In the winter, when the soil is full of moisture, freezing will occur and the expansion will put considerable pressure on the part which extends above the top of the structure. This pressure could be great enough to cause leaking problems or even structural damage. If the built-up part is concrete block construction instead of poured concrete, the chances of leakage and structural damage might be even greater.

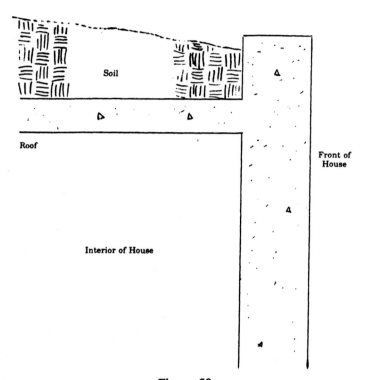

Figure 60

It appears that a good way to avoid this problem would be not to have any part of the front wall extending above the top of the structure, and to let the roof extend out over the front wall. In order to hold the soil on top, some sort of retainer might be made from two-by-eight boards built in a flower-box fashion, or perhaps concrete blocks laid on edge. Whatever is used, it will look rather unattractive until such time as it is covered by vegetation. Hasten the camouflaging job by planting more thickly along this front edge. Since water must be able to drain off the building even on the front, place some pebbles along the inside and at the bottom of the retaining material to allow the rainwater under the retainer to drain easily.

Many people use a mansard roof for the front of their homes. The mansard roof is not so much a roof as a "side" of the house, usually extending from one to three feet above the top of the concrete roof. This will hide the top of the structure, including the unpleasant-looking soil retainer. The mansard roof can extend down as far as you choose and can be positioned at the angle you want (fig. 61).

No matter how often we insist that solar collectors look nice and don't detract from the beauty of a home, most people just don't agree. If you are going to go solar on your underground home, why not use the collector plates as your mansard roof? These roofs can be set at an angle pretty close to the angle at which the collectors should be set and with this method won't stand out like a sore thumb.

A rain trough along the front edge should be installed behind the mansard roof; otherwise the runoff water will rot its soffit.

Let's discuss the exterior of your home with the assumption that you now have the front of the structure the way you want it. One of the big differences you'll find living in an underground home is that there is no back yard for such outside activities as barbecuing. Since there will be no back

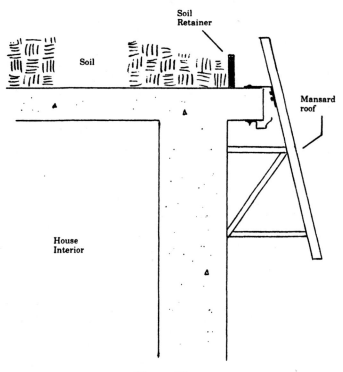

Figure 61

yard, you might need some comparable place on your lot or acreage. One way to gain privacy is by obstructing the view of outsiders with either vegetation or fencing. You may have your own ideas, but figure 62 offers one method of gaining some privacy.

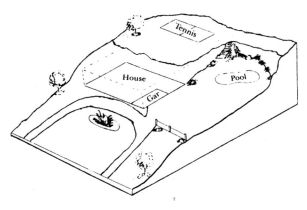

Figure 62

Little is to be found in the way of written help on landscaping underground homes, so you may do best applying the same landscaping principles as you would for a conventional home.

Most landscape designers seem to agree that the front of a conventional home should not be obstructed by tall trees. As a general principle, the same would be true of an underground home. Since so little of an underground home is open to view, accent that part of the house which is most attractive—the entrance. First, plant low-growing trees so that the front of the house will appear to be on the surface rather than look like the entrance to a cave. If there is an area in front or to the side that needs to be shaded for play or other activities, plant a tree to the south and west of the area so that it will be shaded from the hot summer sun.

Shrubs should be grouped optically to stretch the horizontal lines of the front of the house. Use three or more of the same plant for this purpose. Plant shrubs that do not require frequent and extensive trimming and pruning; these are known as low maintenance shrubs. Examples would be junipers, holly, daphne, rhododendron, etc. Check with a local nurseryman to be sure the shrubs you want will grow in your area. The lower your roof line, the smaller the plant should be. For example, if you have a mansard roof extending down near the ground, you should plant ground-hugging junipers or dwarf plants under it. Taller plants would simply grow up to the soffit of the mansard roof, which would look awkward.

Proper landscaping and cared-for grounds are attractive assets for the underground home owner. One of the best and most inexpensive ways to create a good impression is to have a well-manicured yard. A lawn that is mowed and trimmed regularly cannot help but create a good impression on people passing by. The opposite is true of a ragged, overgrown yard.

While we're thinking about the outside of your home, let's look at the contour of the land. *Always* try to move water away from the structure. The best way to do this is with proper contouring of the surface. There should always be a slope to the roof to hasten the removal of water. If you have built back into a hill, there should be contouring of the area between the hill and your house so that the water will be diverted and bypass the house.

Figure 63
The slope of the surface should be a minimum
of one quarter inch per foot for a distance of at
least ten feet from the walls. When you backfill on your walls, tamp the soil so that the fill
won't sink when the first rain comes.

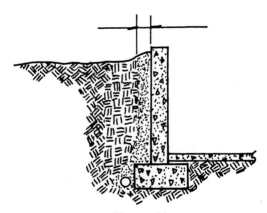

Figure 64
Backfill should be tamped in layers of about
six inches with gravel packed against the outside wall to the surface if there is a serious
water problem where you are building.

Standard Roofs: A Compromise Solution

Especially in the more moderate climate zones, there is much to be said for the idea of using a standard roof on a partially underground (earthen-jacketed) home. This compromise solution between conventional houses and a completely subterranean dwelling makes sense from several points of view: it bypasses considerable resistance among home builders and owners to the concept of underground living, substantially reduces construction problems, and simplifies repairs.

Why would you want to live in a partially underground home? The answer is simple—for the same reason you would want to live in a completely underground home: to save energy costs. The earthen jacket stops all infiltration through the walls, and the temperature a few feet in the earth is far more moderate than the surface temperature. Imagine the weather outside your present home being 15 degrees fahrenheit, with a strong wind blowing. You would have considerable infiltration no matter how much caulking and weather stripping you used, and you would need enough energy to raise the temperature in your home from the 15 degrees outside to approximately 68 degrees, a difference of fifty-three degrees. If you moved your home down into the soil, which at the base of your walls would probably be about 55 degrees fahrenheit, you would need to raise the temperature only about thirteen degrees. You not only have this advantage of having to change the temperature by only a few degrees, but you also have the mass of the structure and the mass of the earth to level out the extremes of the surface temperature. This obviously puts a lot less strain on your heating system—and on your budget.

Because building underground houses with concrete, waterproofed roofs covered with insulation and soil is a strange new concept for most builders in the U.S., they are hesitant to jump into this type of construction. But these same builders would probably not hesitate to build a house surrounded by earth but covered with a standard roof, and people would probably be less hesitant about moving into one. To most people, such a home would not be much different from the one they are already living in—for one thing, an underground home with a standard roof looks much more like a conventional house.

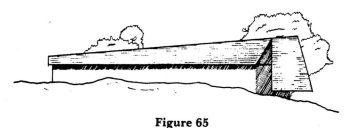

Figure 65
Standard roof on earthen-jacketed home. Soil would be placed against the walls almost all the way to the top.

You might think about a move underground as you would about the first swim of the season. To jump suddenly headfirst into cold water is just too much for most people. Instead, they prefer to enter the water gradually, sticking one foot in first, waiting for a while, placing the other foot in, going in up to the waist, and finally plunging in with their whole bodies. In the same way, although everyone agrees that we are heading toward homes that consume less energy, and that underground homes will head the list of energy misers, there is no stampede to underground living because it seems like too drastic a plunge. If you feel this way, why not try to go underground one step at a time? A standard roof on an earthen-jacketed home is a long step in the right direction.

Construction problems are reduced substantially from those encountered in total underground building. The footing and walls could be built without any significant change from what has been suggested here, but the difficult job of waterproofing a slab or concrete roof would be eliminated. Skilled carpenters routinely build leakproof standard roofs. Insulating the ceiling would be done as it is in most surface homes, with the insulation placed between the joists.

What about the insulative value of standard ceilings compared with those of an earthen-covered structure? Because soil is a poor insulator, its insulative value on the top of a structure can in fact be easily surpassed with manufactured insulation. Soil has an R-value from about 5 to as low as .5 per foot, depending on the type of soil and whether or not it is soaked with moisture. If you have four inches of polystyrene insulation on top of the underground structure with 1-1/2 feet of soil, you have an R-value for the roof varying somewhere between 20 and 30. Compare this with good pour-in insulation ten inches deep in a standard roof, which would give an R-value in excess of 30. Obviously you would not lose any insulative advantage at all; rather, the R-value of a standard roof with insulation above the ceiling can be substantially greater than that of an earth-covered home.

A standard roof would give some attic space for storage and ductwork if the duct system is above the ceiling. But if it is feasible the ducts should be below the ceiling so that you don't have to insulate them. Any heat escaping from the ducts would thus stay in the house.

The moisture problem inside your house would be about the same with a standard roof as with an earth covering. Most new houses now have moisture barriers installed on the walls and ceiling. Roof leaks on a standard roof, however, would be relatively easy to repair.

One word of caution: as the warm air from the interior moves through the ceiling and the insulation, some condensation will take place even if you have a moisture barrier because the air in the attic is much colder than the air from the interior and cannot hold as much moisture. For this reason, you should have good ventilation in the attic area. Ventilation is needed both in winter (to remove moisture) and in summer (to remove hot air). The ventilation will carry the moisture out from the attic and away from the house. Without it, the moisture will enter the insulation and much of its insulative capacity will be lost.

Adequate ventilation can be attained with good prevailing winds, but mechanical ventilation is most desirable. Intake vents should be made in the lower part of the attic and the exit opening should be in the higher part.

Standard roofs have a few disadvantages to consider when making your choice. The exterior noise level might be a little greater with a standard roof, and you would lose some energy savings because of heating and cooling made necessary by extreme surface temperatures. Another loss caused by using a standard roof is of protection from tor-

nadoes and hurricanes: totally underground homes provide the best possible protection from these natural
disasters.

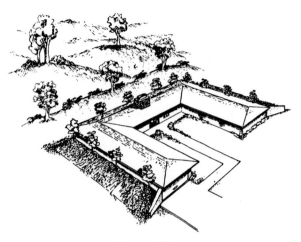

Figure 66
An earthen-jacketed home with standard roof
successfully landscaped—significant energy
savings combined with the look of a conven-
tional home.

An alternative might be to build one closet, including
the ceiling, from reinforced concrete. This is done fre-
quently in new home construction in tornado country.
The closet can be covered with sheetrock or whatever you
are using inside, and would look no different from many
of the other closets in your house—but it would be indestructible. Your family would be cramped in a small, en-
closed space during a storm, but nothing offers more comfort at such a time than being surrounded by solid
concrete.

In addition to removing structural and waterproofing problems, using a conventional roof on an earthen-jacketed home removes the serious psychological barriers raised in some minds by being covered with soil. Acceptance by the general public might therefore be faster, and the going-underground movement ultimately strengthened by this compromise.

Building Sequence

When you decide to build an underground home, there are many things to be done, and many of the steps need to be taken in sequence so that you don't end up spending money undoing what you have already completed. (One example of such a mistake would be to put in sheetrock before you have the electric, telephone, and intercom wiring done.)

Several of the steps could be accomplished at the same time. For example, as soon as the walls are up the inside framing could start, along with such things as waterproofing and insulating the outside walls, installing septic tanks, etc.

Let's go through the various sequences of building an underground home. This sequence of events might differ a little from that of building a conventional home; you might want to alter it slightly to fit your needs. Let's build this underground home right in the middle of the United States, in the great state of Kansas. Most people think of Kansas as being all flat wheatland, but there are some beautiful slopes there that would be ideal for an underground home.

1. Decide on the size you want your house to be and the arrangement of its rooms. This in itself can be a major problem because the natural trend is toward smaller homes because of what may be high initial building costs. To go to a smaller home obviously requires that family members give up a certain amount of space they have previously enjoyed. (Not only is it difficult to get your family to be satisfied with less space, but there will be no back yard where equipment like lawn mowers, rototillers and tools are usually kept.) Our decision is to have three bedrooms, two baths, a fireplace in the den, a kitchen, and a study. The part of the house built into the hill will be round. You can enlarge the house as much as you want by increasing the size of the circle or by decreasing the square or rectangular cutout for the front. We wanted a fairly large cutout so that we could have more windows.

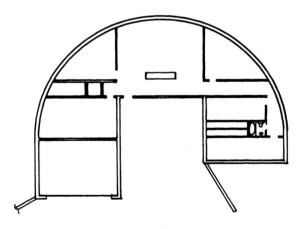

Figure 67
Floor plan agreed upon by family members.

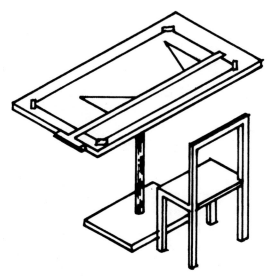

Figure 68
2. Go to an architect or builder and have your ideas put on paper. These are your house plans and will be used throughout the building process. Secure building permits.

Building codes establish construction requirements that promote public safety and health through insistence on structural strength and stability, means of egress, adequate light and ventilation, and protection of life and property from fire and hazards incident to the design, construction, and alteration of buildings and structures. Those are fancy words that mean you should check with the governmental body (usually the city) that establishes building codes in the community where you live. Check with a local builder to find out where to go. Unfortunately, building requirements vary from place to place. Many communities have adopted some of the national codes, and in some small towns and rural communities there may be no building codes at all. Even in a community with no code, your builder will have to comply with certain building requirements if he is utilizing federally sponsored programs for financing.

3. Select and buy your building site. This step may have been done long ago. Most people who want to go underground look for hills or slopes which will allow a southern exposure if only one side of the house is being exposed. Check for a source of good fresh water, from a municipal source or from freshwater sand. Neighbors will let you know what is available. If you have not bought your proposed building site, your house orientation means a lot. First and foremost, you want a hill with a good southern exposure for your windows. A good view is also very important. Be sure that what you see when you look out of those windows is what you want to see. Finally, the prevailing winds are a consideration. The topography can change their direction, so consider the matter carefully (fig. 69).

4. The site has been purchased, so drill your test holes to determine whether or not there is a high water table. If there is, move over a distance and see if you can get out of the high water table area. If the owner will permit you to test, this should be determined before you buy the property. The test should be done during the rainy season because some shallow water aquifers fill up only during the wet part of the year.

5. The drill test shows no abnormal water problem, so excavate to the desired level.

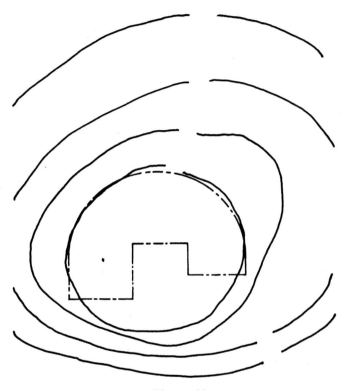

Figure 69
Topographical map of area where the house is to be
built. You can obtain a topographical map of your area
by contacting the U.S. Geological Survey nearest you.

6. Orient the house. Place the forms for footing. Check with your plumber so that arrangements can be made for sleeves to be placed through the footings and sewer and waterlines. This is also a good time to place the sleeves for air vents for the fireplace, etc.

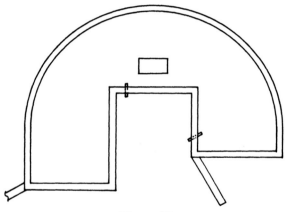

Figure 70

Note that there are footings for the wings of the house (to retain the soil) and the fireplace. The footing plan should also provide for drains.

7. Pour the footings. Be sure there are footings for the fireplace and house wings (retaining walls).

8. Build the walls (using concrete blocks) or pour them (after rebars and forms are up) (fig. 71).
9. Place the plumbing (sewer, waterlines, and drains). Put in an air pipe to feed air to the fireplace.

Figure 71

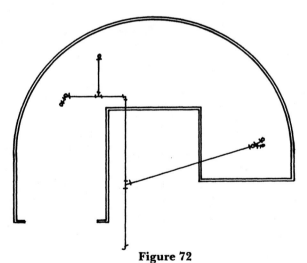

Figure 72
Drawing of house plumbing requirements.

10. Haul gravel or coarse sand and place it over the plumbing.
11. Install waterproofing material and place insulation around the periphery of the floor, which is exposed to the surface temperature.
12. Pour the slab.
13. Waterproof the outside walls.
14. Place drains around the outside of the structure and cover them with rocks or coarse gravel.
15. Insulate the outside of the walls. If water is a threat, use small round rocks (so damage won't occur to the insulation) against the structure for at least twelve inches, and within six inches of the surface. Backfill so there won't be any settling when it rains (fig. 73).

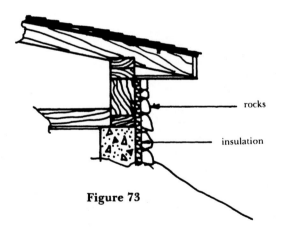

rocks

insulation

Figure 73

16. Frame the interior walls, including the wall for the front part of the house which will be exposed to weather. Use six-inch studs on the front walls so that six-inch insulation can be used between the studs.
17. Construct the frame for the roof (if it is a standard roof) and install the roofing.
18. Complete the home as you would any conventional house. The front of the house could take on any appearance you desire; figure 74 offers one possibility.

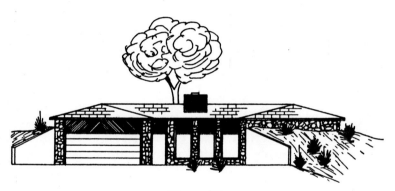

Figure 74

Conclusion

We are still in the infancy stage in the development of underground homes. Such houses will generally become more acceptable with the passage of time. Technology on their construction will improve, and the construction costs will go down.

If the construction costs on subterranean homes become considerably lower than on conventional homes, watch for a building boom underground, with moneylenders eager to lend mortgage money not only because the houses are being accepted by the public, but because they are practically indestructible. Little damage can be done by a fire and the best a tornado can do is suck out a few windows, so little—if any—insurance will be needed. Maintenance is practically nil, and the energy required for temperature moderation is significantly reduced. With all these advantages, why not own one?

Even the military is edging into the underground business (schools and industry have been going underground for some time now). The U.S. Army is planning a terratecture project at Texarkana, Texas, in an effort to reduce the cost of heating and cooling its facilities. This area is the army's energy showcase, and the subterranean project is one of its several experimental demonstrations. If the terratecture project results in substantial savings in heating and cooling costs, get ready for a large part of the military's facilities being moved underground in many locations.

Building an underground home is no job for a novice. Concrete is extremely heavy for its volume and you should not experiment by trying to build an eight-foot concrete wall unless you know what you are doing. Even if you are a pretty good do-it-yourselfer, have the shell built by an experienced builder and then start to work yourself. There will be plenty of work left. Enjoy it.

Reference Material

Brann, Donald R. *Concrete Work Simplified.* New York: Directions Simplified, Inc., 1973.

Calvert, Terri. "The Solartron Prefabricated Earth-Sheltered Home." *Mother Earth News* May/June 1979: 157–59.

Clearinghouse for Earth Covered Buildings. "Earth Covered Shelters: an Overview." Arlington, Texas: School of Architecture and Environmental Design, The University of Texas at Arlington, a free fact sheet. Include a stamped, addressed envelope.

Dean, Andrea O. "Underground Architecture." *AIA Journal* April 1978: 34–51.

Dempewolff, Richard F. "Underground Housing." *Science Digest* November 1975: 40–54.

"Going Underground." *The New York Times* March 22, 1979.

"Going Underground." *Progressive Architecture* April 1976: 138–51.

Gorman, James. "The Earth's the Ceiling: There's a Change of Direction in Architecture and Building." *Sciences* March/April 1976: 16–20.

"Hey! Underground Housing Seminars Are Now Available." *Mother Earth News* May/June 1978: 58.

Labs, Kenneth. "The Architectural Use of Underground Space." Master's Thesis, Washington University, 1975. Reprint available from author, 147 Livingston, New Haven, Ct. 06511.

Labs, Kenneth. "Terratecture: The Underground Design Movement of the 1970s." *Landscape Architecture* May 1977:244–49.

"Living Underground." *Newsweek* June 5, 1978:106–7.

Martindale, David. "New Homes Revive the Ancient Art of Living Underground." *Smithsonian* February 1979: 96–104.

Merritt, Frederick S. *Building Construction Handbook.* New York: McGraw-Hill Book Co., 1975.

Moore, Kenneth. "Coober Pedy: Opal Capital of Australia's Outback." *National Geographic* October 1976.

Moreland, Frank, ed. "Earth Covered Buildings: Technical Notes." National Technical Information Service. 1979.

————. *Earth Covered Buildings and Settlements.* National Technical Information Service, 1979.

————. *Alternatives in Energy Conservation: The Use of Earth Covered Buildings.* National Science Foundation Research Applications Directorate. 1979.

Oehler, Mike. *The $50 & Up Underground House Book.* Bonners Ferry, Idaho: Mole Publishing Company, 1978.

Olin, Harold B., Schmidt, John L., and Lewis, Walter H. *Construction Principles, Materials and Methods.* Chicago, Illinois: The Institute of Financial Education and Interstate Printers and Publishers, Inc., 1975.

"The Paul Isaacson Family Lives in the House of the Future." *Mother Earth News* March/April 1978:101–3.

"The Plowboy Interview: Andy Davis." *Mother Earth News* July/August 1977:18–28.

Rickman, Gary A. and Bennett, Leonard E. *Go Underground and Save.*

Roy, Robert L. *Underground Houses: How to Build a Low-Cost Home.* New York: Sterling, 1979.

"See! Passively Heated Underground Houses Can Be Beautiful Too!" *Mother Earth News* May/June 1978: 101–3.

Smay, V. Elaine. "PS Leisure-Home Plan: Underground Solar House." *Popular Science* December 1978: 86–7.

"Underground Houses—Low Fuel Bills, Low Maintenance, Privacy, Security." *Popular Science* April 1977: 84–89.

"Underground Movement Widens: A Look at Six Subsurface Buildings Along with Some Ideas and Techniques." *AIA Journal* November 1978: 34–49.

Underground Space, 1976. Bimonthly journal published by Pergamon Press.

Underground Space Center, University of Minnesota. *Earth Sheltered Housing Design; Guidelines, Examples and References.* New York: Van Nostrand Reinhold Company, 1978.

Wells, Malcolm B. "Editorial: Environmental Impact." *Progressive Architecture* June 1974: 59–63.

———. "Underground Architecture." *CoEvolution Quarterly* Fall, 1976.

———. *Underground Designs.* Published by the author, 1977.

Wolf, Ray. "The Good Feeling of Living in the Earth; There's an Architectural Revolution Underfoot for Some Very Sound Reasons." *Organic Gardening* December 1978: 58–65.

"Your Next House Could Have a Grass Roof." *Popular Mechanics* March 1977: 78–81.

Index

Notes

Notes

Notes

Notes

Notes

DATE DUE

NOV 0 4 2001

P